Color Quest Color by Number Animals Jumbo Adult Coloring Book for Stress Relief

By Color Questopia

Thank you
for your purchase!

**Claim your FREE digital copy of our
Highlight Reel Color By Number Book:**

Check out our website: colorquestopia.com

**Join our Facebook group:
facebook.com/colorquestopia**

Follow us on Instagram: @colorquestopia

**Did you enjoy this book?
Please leave us a review!**

https://geni.us/cqreview

Color By Number Tips

1. **Relax and have fun**
   Let your cares slip away as you color the images. Take your time.
   Coloring is a meditative activity and there's no wrong way to do it.
   Feel free to color as you listen to music, watch TV, lounge in bed- do
   whatever relaxes you most! You can also color while you're out and
   about- on the train or at a cafe- take the book with you anywhere you
   go. Coloring is therapeutic and is great for stress relief and relaxation!

2. **Colors corresponding to each number are shown on the back
   cover of the book**
   Each number corresponds to a color shown on the back of the book.
   You can match the color as closely as you like- but feel free to change
   the color or the shade if you don't have the exact color match- that's
   totally fine. Although this is a color by number book, it's completely
   okay to get creative and color the images with whichever colors you
   like and have. The numbers are there to be a guide and to allow you
   to color without having to focus your energy on choosing colors.

3. **Choose your coloring tools**
   Everyone has their favorite coloring markers, crayons, pencils, pens-
   even paints! Feel free to color with any tool that you like! If you
   choose markers or paints, we recommend putting a blank sheet of
   paper or cardboard behind each image, so that your colors don't run
   onto the next image.

Enjoy!

1. Light Orange

2. Brown

3. Gray

4. Light Yellow

5. Light Brown

6. Green

7. Light green

8. Army Green

9. Dark green

10. Light Red

11. Blue

12. Orange

13. Red

14. Pink

15. Yellow

16. Dark blue

17. Sky blue

1. Blue
2. Dark Blue
3. Sky Blue
4. Black
5. Light blue
6. Navy blue
7. Yellow
8. Orange
9. Red
10. Army Green
11. Dark Brown
12. Medium brown
13. green
14. Pink
15. Medium green
16. Dark orange
17. Light Brown
18. Neon Green
19. Dark green
20. Light green

1. Black

2. Gray

3. Medium Brown

4. Brown

5. Dark Brown

6. Light Brown

7. Light Yellow

8. Light Orange

9. Orange

10. Medium Green

11. Light Green

12. Army Green

13. Dark Blue

14. Blue

15. Navy Blue

16. Baby Blue

17. Sky Blue

1. Black

2. Navy Blue

3. Light Violet

4. Violet

5. Dark Violet

6. Red

7. Light Pink

8. Pink

9. Dark Pink

10. Light Red

11. Yellow

12. Dark Red

13. Light Orange

14. Hot Pink

15. Orange

16. Purple

17. Dark Green

18. Green

19. Light Green

20. Sky Blue

21. Medium Blue

22. Brown

23. Light Brown

24. Dark Brown

1. Black
2. Light Yellow
3. Light Gray
4. Dark Gray
5. Light Green
6. Baby Blue
7. Dark Blue
8. Dark Yellow
9. Gray
10. Dark Green
11. Green
12. Army Green
13. Yellow
14. Blue
15. Light Blue
16. Sky Blue
17. Medium Blue

1. **Black**

2. **Light Gray**

3. **Gray**

4. **Dark Brown**

5. **Light Violet**

6. **Orange**

7. **Light Yellow**

8. **Dark Orange**

9. **Brown**

10. **Dark Violet**

11. **Medium Purple**

12. **Green**

13. **Light Green**

14. **Neon Green**

15. **Yellow**

16. **Army Green**

17. **Violet**

18. **Dark Gray**

19. **Sky Blue**

20. **Light Pink**

1. Black

2. Dark Brown

3. Red

4. Light Yellow

5. Beige

6. Light Orange

7. Dark Yellow

8. Light Brown

9. Medium Brown

10. Dark Orange

11. Orange

12. Light Brown

13. Medium Orange

14. Navy Blue

15. Violet

16. Green

17. Baby Blue

1. Black

2. Hot Pink

3. Pink

4. Medium Pink

5. Dark Red

6. Orange

7. Red

8. Light Pink

9. Beige

10. Yellow

11. Violet

12. Light Gray

13. Light Orange

14. Light Brown

15. Dark Brown

16. Dark Red

17. Medium Orange

18. Dark Orange

19. Brown

20. Light Yellow

21. Green

22. Medium Brown

23. Sky Blue

1. Black

2. Dark Brown

3. Dark Gray

4. Gray

5. Light Red

6. Army Green

7. Light Gray

8. Hot Pink

9. Brown

10. Beige

11. Dark Orange

12. Orange

13. Medium Gray

14. Soft Violet

15. Light Brown

16. Light Orange

17. Sky Blue

18. Navy Blue

19. Medium Purple

20. Red

1. Black
2. Dark Brown
3. Brown
4. Dark Orange
5. Beige
6. Orange
7. Light Gray
8. Medium Orange
9. Light Orange
10. Medium Pink
11. Gray
12. Light Yellow
13. Light Green
14. Medium Red
15. Violet
16. Light Blue
17. Sky Blue
18. Bright Orange
19. Hot Pink
20. Light Green

1. Red

2. Yellow

3. Lemon Yellow

4. Light Yellow

5. Dark Yellow

6. Light Green

7. Army Green

8. Orange

9. Violet

10. Black

11. Dark Green

12. Medium Gray

13. Dark Gray

14. Light Pink

15. Medium Green

16. Blue

17. Sky blue

18. Green

19. Brown

20. Neon Green

21. Light gray

22. Navy blue

22. Beige

1. Dark Orange
2. Dark Violet
3. Dark Brown
4. Dark Blue
5. Light Yellow
6. Black
7. Yellow
8. Light Orange
9. Navy Blue
10. Blue
11. Dark Blue
12. Medium Green
13. Orange
14. Beige
15. Neon Green

16. Army Green
17. Light Green
18. Green
19. Medium Orange
20. Dark Green
21. Medium Yellow

1. Black
2. Dark Brown
3. Medium Brown
4. Dark Red
5. Brown
6. Light Brown
7. Light Orange
8. Light Red
9. Beige
10. Green
11. Neon Green
12. Army Green
13. Medium Green
14. Light Green
15. Dark Green
16. Navy Blue
17. Sky Blue
18. Orange
19. Yellow

1. Chocolate

2. Medium Gray

3. Light Gray

4. Beige

5. Dark Gray

6. Gray

7. Soft Violet

8. Brown

9. Red

10. Navy Blue

11. Yellow

12. Orange

13. Light Blue

14. Sky Blue

15. Light Violet

16. Violet

17. Pink

18. Green

1. Black

2. Blue

3. Army Green

4. Neon Green

5. Medium Green

6. Dark Yellow

7. Dark Green

8. Light Green

9. Green

10. Beige

11. Red

12. Yellow

13. Light Violet

14. Orange

15. Sky Blue

16. Baby Blue

17. Violet

1. Black
2. Light Violet
3. Dark Blue
4. Light Pink
5. Dark Brown
6. Gray
7. Light Gray
8. Light Brown
9. Dark Red
10. Soft Violet
11. Orange
12. Medium Gray
13. Light Yellow
14. Dark Pink
15. Light Red
16. Brown
17. Dark Yellow
18. Green
19. Yellow
20. Sky Blue

1. Black

2. Dark Gray

3. Dark Brown

4. Gray

5. Soft Violet

6. Light Gray

7. Dark Gray

8. Medium Gray

9. Light Orange

10. Light Yellow

11. Army Green

12. Neon Green

13. Light Green

14. Green

15. Sky Blue

16. Baby Blue

17. Light Blue

18. Blue

19. Dark Blue

20. Navy Blue

1. Chocolate

2. Dark Brown

3. Brown

4. Medium Brown

5. Light Brown

6. Light Yellow

7. Beige

8. Light Gray

9. Medium Gray

10. Army Green

11. Neon Green

12. Light Green

13. Baby Blue

14. Light Blue

15. Blue

16. Yellow

17. Orange

1. Black

2. Medium Green

3. Green

4. Light Green

5. Neon Green

6. Yellow

7. Brown

8. Light Brown

9. Red

10. Orange

11. Army Green

12. Dark Green

13. Beige

14. Light Blue

15. Light Pink

16. Navy Blue

17. Baby Blue

18. Sky Blue

19. Blue

20. Violet

1. Black

2. Brown

3. Red

4. Light Green

5. Medium Green

6. Army Green

7. Yellow

8. Beige

9. Neon Green

10. Medium Brown

11. Light Brown

12. Dark Green

13. Light Yellow

14. Light Orange

15. Blue

16. Baby Blue

17. Green

Easy Design
Adult Color By Number
Jumbo Coloring Book of Large Print
Flowers, Birds, and Butterflies

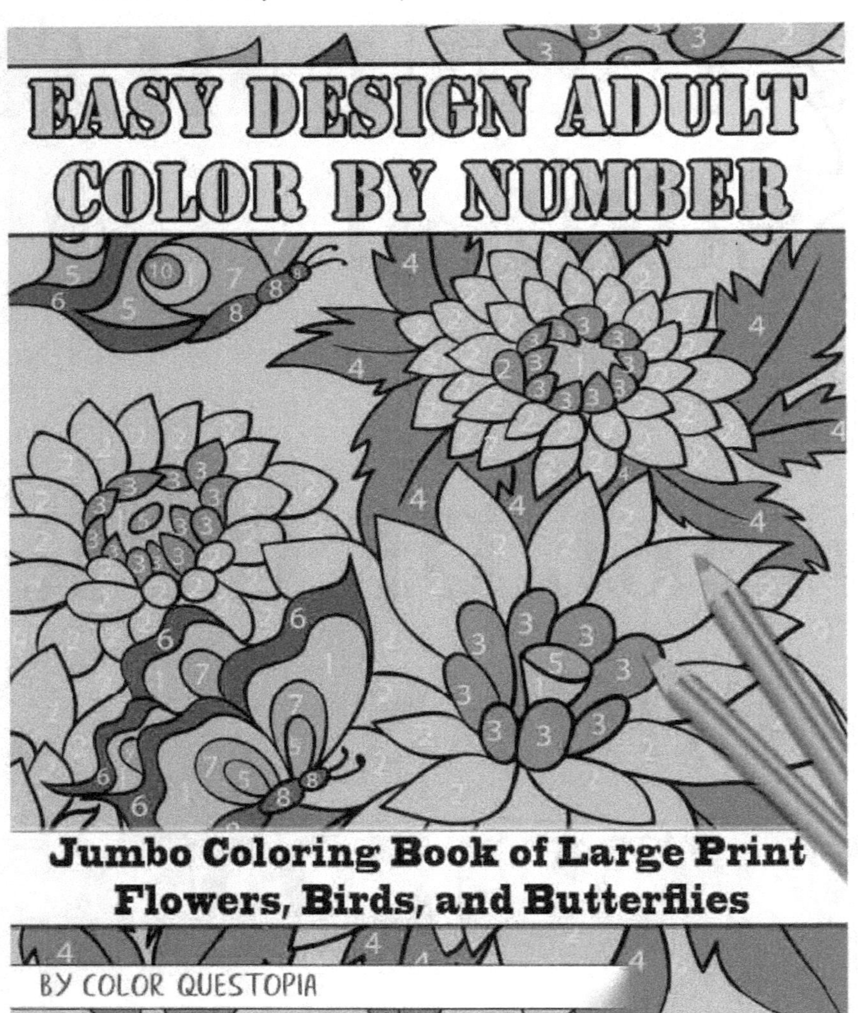

1. Light Red   2. Red   3. Green   4. Yellow   5. Orange   6. Light Brown
7. Brown   8. Sky Blue

New York
Mosaic Color by Number
Coloring Book for Adults

1. Orange

2. Yellow

3. Light Yellow

4. Dark Red

5. Brown

6. Sky Blue

7. Blue

8. Light Pink

9. Light Orange

10. Red

11. Dark Brown

12. Dark Orange

13. Dark Gray

14. Light Gray

15. Light Violet

16. Violet

17. Light Purple

Fanciful Fox
Mosaic Adult Color by Number Book
Adult Coloring Book for Stress Relief
and Relaxation

1. Black

2. Dark Brown

3. Light Yellow

4. Yellow

5. Orange

6. Medium Brown

7. Light Brown

8. Dark Yellow

9. Brown

10. Neon Green

11. Army Green

12. Medium Green

13. Green

14. Dark Green

15. Light Green

16. Sky Blue

17. Blue

Country Farm Scenes
Nature, Animal, and Easy Designs
Adult Coloring Book
Color By Number For Adults

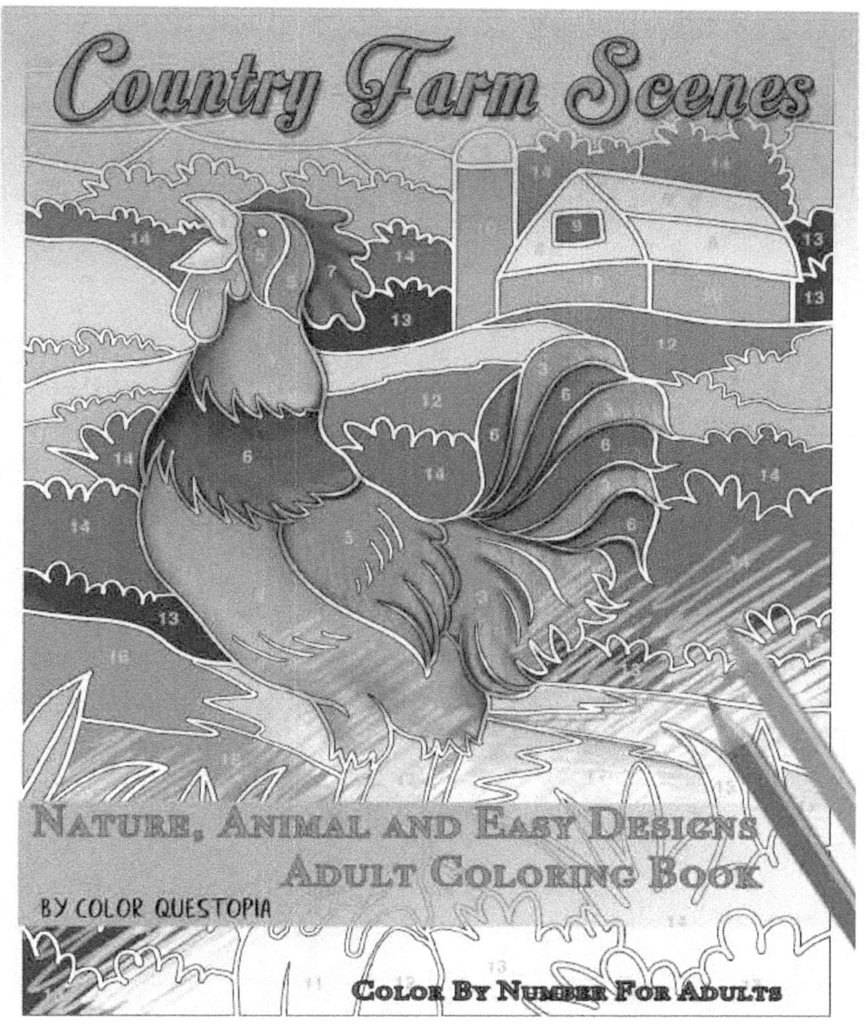

1. Dark Brown

2. Dark Orange

3. Orange

4. Red

5. Dark Red

6. Soft Violet

7. Violet

8. Yellow

9. Light Brown

10. Brown

11. Dark Green

12. Green

13. Medium Green

14. Light Green

15. Neon Green

16. Blue

17. Light Blue

Horses Jumbo Adult Coloring Book
Horses and Ponies Grazing and Racing
Color by Number

1. Dark brown

2. Dark Orange

3. Brown

4. Red

5. Medium Brown

6. Dark Orange

7. Orange

8. White

9. Light brown

10. Light Gray

11. Light Orange

12. Dark Yellow

13. Black

14. Army green

15. Light Red

16. Dark Red

17. Sky blue

18. Blue

19. Dark blue

20. Light blue

Please
Leave
Us
A Review
On Amazon